LOW CALORIE

HOME COOKING

First published in Great Britain by Simon & Schuster UK Ltd, 2005
A Viacom Company

Simon & Schuster UK Ltd
Africa House
64–78 Kingsway
London
WC2B 6AH

1 3 5 7 9 10 8 6 4 2

Design: **Fiona Andreanelli**
Food photography: **Juliet Piddington**
Home economist: **Kim Morphew**
Stylist for food photography: **Helen Trent**
Copy-editor: **Nicole Foster**
Proofreader: **Michèle Clarke**
Nutritionist: **Jill Foster**
Indexer: **Deborah Savage**
Printed and bound in China

ISBN 0 74325 976 9

Best-kept Secrets of the Women's Institute

LOW CALORIE HOME COOKING

Jenny Kieldsen

SIMON & SCHUSTER
A VIACOM COMPANY

ACKNOWLEDGEMENTS

I would like to say a huge **Thank You** to Tracy Strain, Head of Courses at Denman College, who put my name forward to write this book; and also, to my friends, and past students, who have always encouraged me and said "you should write a book". Lastly, a big Thank You to Polly Tyrer and Gay Baker for their expertise and advice.

CONTENTS

INTRODUCTION

'Low calorie cooking' does not mean that you can't still enjoy wonderful food. Just that you need to eat the correct amount of calories for your lifestyle, not any extra – because this is when you put on weight. With a little more care when choosing ingredients, and some different cooking methods, you could really change your diet and your waistline. Read on. . .

What is a calorie? Strictly speaking it is the amount of heat required to raise the temperature of 1 gram of water by 1 degree Celsius. The dietician's 'calorie' is, strictly, the kilocalorie (kcal) – 1000 of the scientist's calories – but the 'kilo' has been dropped in popular usage.

Different foods are used by the body to produce different amounts of energy – which is why a small piece of chocolate can have many more calories than a similar-sized piece of lettuce. In order to lose weight you need to eat fewer calories per day. The recommended amount differs from person to person, depending on how active/tall/old you are. The basic fact to bear in mind is that you need to consume the same amount of calories as the amount of energy that you expend, any extra will be excess weight! The general guidelines below will help you with a calorie-controlled diet.

An average adult man needs between 2,500 and 3,000 calories per day.

An average adult woman needs between 2,000 and 2,500 calories per day.

That can begin to seem rather complicated. So here is a book of recipes that are already calorie counted. They are easy to follow with simple and straightforward instructions – and taste far nicer than any supermarket 'low calorie' meals, which are often surprisingly high in fat and additives. This is not a diet cookery book, but it is a guide to healthy eating using low calorie ingredients.

Most of these recipes can be eaten for any meal at any time of the day. It is a good idea to have the key ingredients ready at home so you can rustle up something quickly. Keep a good store cupboard of basics and you will always have something at hand ready to cook.

There are many ways to make food taste good without using lots of butter or frying in huge amounts of oil. Instead, buy low fat yogurts, low fat crème fraîche, and half fat cheeses and spreads. Use cooking spray oils, available in the supermarket, or a pastry brush to grease a pan. Non-stick pots and frying pans radically reduce the amount of oil needed. Add a little water to your pan or wok and 'steam' what you are cooking. Covering the pan with a lid also helps. Try to bear these details in mind next time you are following a recipe.

Salt is naturally present in small amounts in most foods, and a worryingly large amount is added to the ready-prepared meals available in our supermarkets. It's best to avoid adding too much salt, and concentrate on introducing flavour in other ways. Use fresh garlic and ginger, cider vinegar, wine, honey, chillies, cumin and coriander seeds, curry powder, fresh herbs (especially coriander) and Chinese five spice powder. Experiment and you will find new flavours that suit you and your family. Worcestershire and soy sauces are good too, though they do contain some salt.

Bread, especially home made, is wonderful with food but the temptation to pile on the butter is always there. Try making your own Melba toast (page 14) and croutons (page 25). These add great texture and crunch, and are easy to make and store.

The recipes in this book cover most aspects of a daily diet so can be incorporated into a completely calorie controlled regime or they can be used at random for a generally healthier way of eating.

A final footnote: breakfast is really the most important meal of the day. If you begin the day well fed you are less likely to start snacking mid-morning. Either porridge or muesli and fruit would be good choices.

Soup is an excellent standby, so it's worth making extra and freezing it in portions. It is then ready to use when there is nothing else in the cupboard. The Minestrone is completely fat free – try serving it with Bruschetta (page 20) for a complete meal. Gazpacho is quick and fat free too. It also tastes authentic, particularly made in the summer with fresh peppers and English cucumbers.

SOUPS & STARTERS

Do try my Low Cal Prawn Cocktail: 1970s' food is very fashionable at the moment, and this modern version makes a good light lunch or a dinner party starter.

SERVES 4
PREPARATION & COOKING TIME:
20 minutes + 1¼ hours cooking
FREEZING: recommended

MINESTRONE

This is a very simple and **authentic-tasting** recipe. Using a food processor to grate the vegetables makes it even easier, but you can grate by hand if you like. You will find soup pasta in the supermarket, or you can use small pieces of broken spaghetti instead.

PER SERVING: 153 calories, 1 g fat

I small turnip or swede
2 carrots
I potato, peeled
400 g can of whole or chopped tomatoes
I large onion, sliced finely
2 celery sticks, shredded finely
3-4 Savoy or green cabbage leaves, shredded finely
2 fresh bay leaves
I teaspoon dried basil
I vegetable stock cube
75g (2³/₄ oz) 'tiny' soup pasta
salt and freshly ground black pepper
freshly grated half fat Parmesan cheese, to serve

1 Grate the turnip or swede, carrots and potato, and put into a large saucepan filled with 850 ml (1½ pints) of water. Whizz the tomatoes in a food processor, and add to the saucepan.
2 Add all the other vegetables, the herbs, seasoning and stock cube and simmer slowly with a lid on for 1 hour, stirring occasionally.
3 Add the pasta, and cook for a further 8–10 minutes. Remove the bay leaves, taste to check the seasoning, and serve with grated Parmesan sprinkled over.

SERVES 4
PREPARATION & COOKING TIME:
10 minutes + 20 minutes cooking
FREEZING: recommended

SERVES 4
PREPARATION & COOKING TIME:
10 minutes + 30 minutes cooking
FREEZING: recommended

VERY GREEN PEA SOUP

WATERCRESS SOUP

This soup uses frozen peas. It has a **lovely bright colour**, and is quick and easy to make.

The fresh **peppery flavour** of watercress really comes through in this simple recipe. It is also very good served cold, though you may prefer to make the consistency thinner by adding a little more water and milk.

PER SERVING: 107 calories, 4 g fat

PER SERVING: 96 calories, 3 g fat

25 g (1 oz) low fat spread
1 onion, chopped roughly
450 g (1 lb) frozen peas
salt and freshly ground black pepper
small sprig of fresh mint
1 chicken stock cube

15 g (^{1}/$_2$ oz) low fat spread
1 onion, chopped roughly
1 potato, peeled and chopped roughly
1 bunch of watercress, chopped roughly
300 ml (^{1}/$_2$ pint) semi skimmed milk
1 vegetable stock cube
salt and freshly ground black pepper

1   Melt the spread in a saucepan, add the onion and lightly fry for 2–3 minutes. Add the peas (still frozen) and stir well until thawed.
2   Add 150 ml (^{1}/$_4$ pint) water, salt, pepper and the mint and bring to the boil. Cover, turn the heat very low and simmer for 12 minutes until the onion is soft. Remove the mint.
3   Cool for 15 minutes, then pour into a food processor and whizz until smooth. Return to the saucepan with 425 ml (^{3}/$_4$ pint) water and the crumbled stock cube.
4   Bring to the boil, stirring well to dissolve the stock cube. Taste to check the seasoning before serving.

1   Melt the fat in a saucepan, and gently fry the onion for 2 minutes. Add the potato and watercress, stir to mix, and pour over about 150 ml (^{1}/$_4$ pint) water so that the vegetables are just covered.
2   Season with salt and pepper, cover with a tightly fitting lid and cook very slowly for about 15–20 minutes until the potato is soft. Leave to cool for 10 minutes.
3   Whizz in a food processor or liquidiser with the milk until smooth. Return to the saucepan and add 300 ml (^{1}/$_2$ pint) water and the stock cube.
4   Bring up to the boil, stirring well, and taste to check the seasoning before serving.

SERVES 4
PREPARATION & COOKING TIME:
I hour
FREEZING: not recommended

PER SERVING: 327 calories, 17 g fat

8 peppers, halved and de-seeded
4 tablespoons extra virgin olive oil
2 large sprigs of fresh rosemary,
broken into 8
salt and freshly ground black pepper
8 slices of thin or medium sliced bread
(white, wholemeal or granary)

Use an assortment of **different coloured peppers**, red, yellow, green or orange, for this recipe. Leaving the skins on adds to the texture and makes the cooking very simple. The peppers also make wonderful sandwiches, with no need for any spread on the bread. Make as much Melba toast at a time as you can manage - it is so moreish. Once cooled it can be stored in an airtight tin.

1   Cut each of the pepper halves into three, and remove the white pith. Put the pieces of pepper into the bottom of the grill pan or on a shallow tray that will fit under the grill.
2   Pour over the oil, and mix well so that all the peppers are coated. Tuck in the rosemary, season with salt and pepper, and put under a high grill.
3   Cook until the peppers are blackened and 'floppy', turning with tongs to cook both sides. This will take approximately 30–40 minutes. Remove the cooked peppers to a dish and leave to cool with all the cooking oils. Remove the rosemary stalks.
4   To make the melba toast, have ready a sharp bread knife and a large chopping board. Using the grill, toast two slices of bread on both sides. Immediately cut off all the crusts, and then cut through the middle of the slices to make four slices (this is quite easy as the toast is hot). Put the four slices back under the grill, cut side up. Watch carefully – they will brown and curl up very quickly. Remove immediately and cool. Repeat with the remaining bread slices.
5   Serve the peppers either warm or cold in the cooking oil (add extra if you like), sliced into thin strips with the Melba toast. The peppers can be cooked the day before and stored in the fridge.

ROASTED PEPPERS WITH ROSEMARY & MELBA TOAST

SERVES 4
PREPARATION & COOKING TIME:
overnight soaking + 15 minutes
+ 50 minutes cooking
FREEZING: not recommended

PER SERVING: 222 calories, 13 g fat

Homemade houmous is definitely worth making: while supermarket brands are very good, your own version will taste fabulous, with a **lovely nutty flavour**. For a change, do try serving the houmous just warm, as soon as it's made.

HOUMOUS WITH BLACK OLIVES

125 g (4¹/₂ oz) dried chick peas, soaked in
cold water overnight
1 or 2 garlic cloves
juice of ¹/₂ lemon
1 tablespoon tahini (sesame seed paste)
1 tablespoon good quality olive oil
salt and freshly ground black pepper

TO SERVE:
black olives
olive oil, for drizzling
wholemeal pitta bread, toasted

1 Put the drained chick peas into a saucepan and cover with water. Bring to the boil, cover and simmer for 40–50 minutes until just soft.
2 Leave to cool for 10 minutes, drain, and reserve 150 ml (¹/₄ pint) of the cooking liquid. Put the chick peas, reserved cooking liquid, garlic, lemon juice, tahini and oil into a food processor.

3 Whizz until smooth, add salt and pepper, whizz again, and taste to check the seasoning. Leave until cold.
4 Spread on one large or four individual white plates, add some olives to each portion and a drizzle of olive oil. Serve with toasted wholemeal pitta bread.

SERVES: 4
PREPARATION TIME: 15 minutes
FREEZING: not recommended

PER SERVING: 98 calories, 4 g fat

Just because everyone makes jokes about prawn cocktail doesn't mean that you should not serve it. Made well, it is still **a wonderful starter**. The Tabasco and gin in this version really 'pep' it up. You can substitute vodka for the gin if you prefer.

LOW CAL PRAWN COCKTAIL

3 tablespoons low calorie mayonnaise
1 tablespoon tomato purée
a few drops of Tabasco sauce
1 tablespoon gin
salt
300 g (10 1/2 oz) frozen prawns, defrosted naturally, and well drained
1 Little Gem or Cos lettuce, shredded
1 tablespoon chopped fresh parsley, to garnish
1 lemon, cut into 4 wedges, to serve

1 Mix together the mayonnaise and tomato purée with a small whisk and stir in the Tabasco, gin and salt. Taste to check the seasoning.
2 Add the prawns to the mayonnaise and mix well.
3 Divide the lettuce between four glasses or small bowls.
4 When you are ready to serve pile the prawns on to the lettuce, sprinkle over the parsley and place a lemon wedge on each bowl.

SERVES 4
PREPARATION & COOKING TIME:
20 minutes + 1 hour marinating
+ 15 minutes cooking
FREEZING: not recommended

PER SERVING: 141 calories, 3 g fat

Pork is very tasty served this simple way, and the mango salsa really **complements the dish**. The recipe makes a good main course for two. It's very important for the mango to be really ripe, so it's worth buying one in advance and leaving it to ripen on a warm windowsill. The flavour is quite different once the fruit is soft and juicy. Satay sticks can be found at supermarkets in the barbecue section. If you are worried that the sticks may burn, wrap a little foil around the bare ends.

FOR THE SATAY:
2 x 175 g (6 oz) boneless pork steaks, trimmed of all fat and gristle
2 tablespoons dark soy sauce
a walnut-sized piece of fresh ginger, peeled and chopped finely
2 garlic cloves, crushed
a good squeeze of lime juice

FOR THE SALSA:
1 small very ripe mango, peeled and chopped finely
1 small fresh red chilli, de-seeded and chopped finely
$^1/_4$ red onion, chopped finely
juice of $^1/_2$ lime
1 tablespoon fresh coriander, chopped finely
salt and freshly ground black pepper

1 Put the steaks between clingfilm and beat with a wooden rolling pin to a thickness of 5 mm ($^1/_4$ inch). Cut into bite size pieces and put into a bowl.
2 Pour over the soy sauce, ginger, garlic and lime juice. Stir to mix well, cover with clingfilm and leave to marinate for 1 hour.
3 Meanwhile, soak eight wooden satay sticks in cold water to prevent burning.
4 While the pork is marinating, prepare the salsa. Mix all the ingredients together, cover with cling film, and allow to stand at room temperature for at least 15 minutes.
5 Thread the pork on to the sticks, taking care not to push the pieces of meat too close together.
6 Cook under a hot grill (or on the barbecue) for 12–15 minutes, turning to brown all sides. Serve on the sticks with the salsa.

PORK SATAY WITH MANGO SALSA

SERVES 4
PREPARATION TIME: 15 minutes + 1 hour chilling
FREEZING: not recommended

QUICK GAZPACHO

Delicious and very quickly made in a liquidiser, this **classic Spanish soup** is also very cooling in the summer.

PER SERVING: 58 calories, 1 g fat

225 g (8 oz) red and green peppers, halved and de-seeded
1 cucumber, peeled
1 or 2 garlic cloves
400 g can of whole tomatoes
salt and freshly ground black pepper

1   Trim all the white pith from the peppers and cut into chunks. Cut the cucumber into chunks.
2   Put half the peppers, cucumber and garlic with the tomatoes into a liquidiser, whizz until smooth, and pour into a bowl. Now add the remaining vegetables plus 200 ml (7 fl oz) water to the liquidiser and whizz again, then add to the bowl.
3   Pour into a serving bowl and stir the soup well to mix. Season with salt and pepper and taste. Chill in the fridge for at least 1 hour. The soup can be served with croutons (page 25).

SERVES 4
PREPARATION & COOKING TIME: 15 minutes
FREEZING: not recommended

BRUSCHETTA

Bruschetta is a very simple and **rustic dish**. Eat as a starter or as a quick snack, where it makes an interesting and 'crunchy' alternative to a sandwich.

PER SERVING: 140 calories, 3 g fat

1 small French stick or a small ciabatta loaf
1 garlic clove
a little good quality olive oil
25 g (1 oz) fresh basil leaves
4 Italian plum tomatoes (on the vine are best for flavour), sliced thinly
salt and freshly ground black pepper

1   Cut the bread in half and split the halves again to make four portions. Grill on both sides until crispy.
2   Remove from the grill and immediately rub the garlic clove over the crusty surfaces, and then sprinkle over a little olive oil.
3   Lay three or four basil leaves on each piece of bread and top with the sliced tomatoes. Season with a little salt and pepper and eat immediately.

SERVES 4
PREPARATION & COOKING TIME: 15 minutes
FREEZING: not recommended

SERVES 4
PREPARATION & COOKING TIME: overnight defrosting
+ 20 minutes + 15 minutes cooking
FREEZING: not recommended

WARM ASPARAGUS WITH BALSAMIC DRESSING

English asparagus is the best, and is in season during May and June, but imported makes a good second choice. Trim the tough ends from the spears, and cut the lengths to fit your saucepan, about 18 cm (7 inches). Don't be put off by thinking that asparagus is difficult to cook – it's not! Use the best balsamic vinegar that you can afford.

PER SERVING: 178 calories, 13 g fat

20 (4–5 per person) asparagus spears, washed and trimmed
2–3 tablespoons walnut or hazelnut oil
2–3 tablespoons balsamic vinegar
50 g (1³/₄ oz) half fat Parmesan cheese, grated into shavings
Melba toast, to serve (page 14)

1   Bring a large saucepan of salted water to the boil, and drop in the asparagus spears, so that they lie lengthways in the pan, all facing the same way. Turn the heat down to a simmer.
2   Cook for about 8 minutes, then test the spears with the point of a sharp knife – they need to be just cooked. Put four layers of kitchen towel on a plate. Remove the asparagus from the pan with a slotted spoon and place on the kitchen towel to drain.
3   Arrange the spears (facing the same way) on four serving plates. Sprinkle over the oil and vinegar, then shave a little Parmesan over each portion, using the coarse blade of the grater. Serve while still warm with Melba toast.

WARM CHICKEN LIVER SALAD

This also makes a **good supper dish** for two people. Using curly endive lettuce adds an interesting flavour and texture.

PER SERVING: 147 calories, 6 g fat

2 x 225 g tubs of frozen chicken livers, defrosted overnight
salt and freshly ground black pepper
1 tablespoon olive oil
125 g (4¹/₂ oz) curly endive or mixed salad leaves
2 tablespoons good quality balsamic vinegar
1 tablespoon chopped fresh parsley

1   Drain the chicken livers in a sieve for 20 minutes, trim well and cut into bite size pieces. Put on kitchen towel to dry and season with salt and pepper.
2   Heat a small non-stick frying pan, add the oil and fry the livers for 8–10 minutes until golden and crispy on all sides.
3   Meanwhile, divide the endive or salad leaves between four plates. Remove the livers from the frying pan with a slotted spoon and scatter over the lettuce.
4   Put the pan back on the heat, add the balsamic vinegar, bring up to the boil and pour the juices over the salad.
5   Sprinkle over the parsley and serve immediately. Fennel flatbread (page 30) would be good to mop up the juices.

All these salads can be served alone, as a light meal, or as an accompaniment to any of the main courses. For extra flavour try rubbing a clove of garlic around the inside of the salad bowl, it works really well if the bowl is made of wood. Do treat yourself to extra virgin olive oil. The taste is so different, and it can be 'splashed' over salads as a final dressing. A little good quality hazelnut or walnut oil is also wonderful just sprinkled

SALADS & SNACKS

over some supermarket mixed leaves. Salads can be made in advance but must never be 'dressed' until the last moment.

The Sweet Potato Chips are a bit different and definitely worth a try. The Fennel Flatbread is very easy to make and can be used to make croutons as well. The Butterbean Dip with Crudités is probably the quickest recipe in the book!

SERVES 4
PREPARATION & COOKING TIME:
40 minutes
FREEZING: not recommended

PER SERVING: 267 calories, 20 g fat

Make double the amount of French dressing. It will keep in the fridge in a screw top jar for at least three weeks.

100 g (3¹/₂ oz) French beans, topped, tailed and halved
2 Little Gem lettuces or 1 Cos lettuce
4 tomatoes, each cut into 8
¹/₂ small onion, sliced very finely
175 g can of tuna in brine, very well drained
2 hard boiled eggs, quartered
8–10 black or green olives
chopped fresh parsley, to serve

FOR THE FRENCH DRESSING:
4 tablespoons olive oil
1 tablespoon cider vinegar or tarragon vinegar
a good pinch of sugar
1 garlic clove, crushed
1 teaspoon French mustard
salt and freshly ground black pepper

1 Bring a small saucepan of water to the boil and add the beans. Bring back to the boil, boil for 1 minute, drain, and immediately rinse in cold water.
2 Wash and chop the lettuce into bite size chunks and arrange on a large serving dish. Add the tomatoes, beans, onion and the tuna, broken into chunks.
3 Lay the eggs and olives on top. Then, with very clean hands, gently mix the salad together.
4 Put all the dressing ingredients into a screw top jar and shake well.
5 When ready to serve, toss with the dressing and sprinkle with parsley.

NIÇOISE SALAD

SERVES 4
PREPARATION & COOKING TIME:
15 minutes + 20 minutes cooking
FREEZING: not recommended

PER SERVING: 99 calories, 5 g fat

No salt is needed because the anchovy essence is very salty. Any extra croutons will keep well in a tin, so **cook more than you need** and use to garnish soups. If you use a Microplane Grater for the Parmesan, the cheese will be very fine, and will go a long way.

2 slices thick wholemeal or granary bread, crusts removed
¹/₂ x 200 g pot of low fat crème fraîche
1 garlic clove, crushed
a squeeze of lemon juice
1 dessertspoon anchovy essence
freshly ground black pepper
1 Cos lettuce or 2 Little Gem lettuces
50 g (2 oz) half fat Parmesan cheese, freshly grated

1 Preheat the oven to Gas Mark 4/electric oven 180°C/fan oven 160°C.
2 To make the croutons, cut the bread into small squares, put on a flat baking sheet and bake for about 20 minutes until completely dry and crispy.
3 Put the crème fraîche in a small bowl and mix in the garlic, lemon juice, anchovy essence and pepper. Taste to check the seasoning.
4 Chop the lettuce roughly and put in a deep bowl. When you are ready to serve, pour over the crème fraîche dressing, mix well and sprinkle over the croutons and Parmesan.

CLASSIC CAESAR SALAD WITH CROUTONS

SERVES 4
PREPARATION TIME: 20 minutes
FREEZING: not recommended

PER SERVING: 150 calories, 9 g fat

This is **a take on the classic** Waldorf salad. I have cut down on the nuts, and substituted French dressing for mayonnaise. Smoked chicken has a really good flavour, but you could substitute cold cooked chicken if preferred.

SMOKED CHICKEN WALDORF

**I head of celery, trimmed and cut into chunks
2 red skinned apples, quartered and cored
50 g (1³/₄ oz) walnut pieces
100 g (3¹/₂ oz) smoked chicken breast, cut into bite size pieces
3 tablespoons French dressing (page 24)
2 tablespoons chopped fresh parsley, to garnish**

1 Put the celery in a large bowl. Cut the apple quarters in half again, and cut each piece into four or five chunks. Add to the celery.

2 Add the walnuts, chicken and French dressing, and stir to mix well. Pile in a pretty dish, sprinkle over the parsley and serve immediately.

SERVES 2 as a main course, 4 as a starter
PREPARATION & COOKING TIME:
10 minutes + 25 minutes cooking
FREEZING: not recommended

WARM LENTIL SALAD

Puy lentils are highly regarded and considered by some to be the best available. You will find them in the supermarket. They are a little more expensive than ordinary lentils but definitely worth paying for. This warm salad is also good when eaten cold.

PER SERVING (X 4): 174 calories, 8 g fat

125 g (4¹/₂ oz) Puy lentils
1 red onion, halved and sliced very thinly
1 tablespoon tarragon vinegar
juice of 1 lime
2 tablespoons olive oil
2 teaspoons ground cumin
1 garlic clove, crushed
salt
2 tablespoons chopped fresh coriander
natural yogurt, to serve

1   Put the lentils in a saucepan and cover with water. Simmer gently for about 20–25 minutes until just soft: they need to retain their shape but not be mushy.
2   Meanwhile, put the onion in a shallow bowl and pour over the vinegar. Cover with clingfilm and leave to marinate for 15 minutes.
3   Put the lime juice, olive oil, cumin, garlic and salt in a large bowl and stir to mix. When the lentils are cooked drain well, and add to the bowl while still hot.
4   Add the onions and vinegar, mix together gently and pile into a serving dish. Sprinkle over the coriander and serve warm with yogurt.

SERVES 4
PREPARATION & COOKING TIME:
Overnight soaking + 1 hour + 15 minutes cooling
FREEZING: not recommended

TUNA & CHICK PEAS

This dish is loosely based on the classic Italian dish *tonno e fagioli* (tuna and beans). The tuna and chick peas partner each other really well. It makes **a great snack dish**, and will keep in the fridge for 2–3 days. In fact, it is almost more tasty the next day.

PER SERVING: 334 calories, 18 g fat

175g (6oz) dried chick peas, soaked in cold water overnight
¹/₂ red onion, finely sliced
grated zest and juice of 1 lemon
4 tablespoons good quality olive oil
185 g can of tuna in brine, well drained
salt and freshly ground black pepper
2 tablespoons chopped fresh parsley

1   Put the drained chick peas in a saucepan, cover with water and simmer for about 45–50 minutes until they are soft but still retain some bite.
2   Meanwhile, put the onion, lemon zest, juice and olive oil in a wide shallow dish. Drain the chick peas and put straight into the dish while still hot. Stir to mix.
3   Season well with salt and pepper, add the tuna and mix together to break up the tuna chunks. Cover and leave to cool. Taste to check the seasoning and sprinkle with chopped parsley.

SERVES 6
PREPARATION & COOKING TIME: 35 minutes + 2 hours setting
FREEZING: not recommended

CUCUMBER MOUSSE WITH PRAWNS

Set in ramekins these make **a good dinner party starter** – or serve in a soufflé dish as a great supper dish for three. Melba toast (page 14) would provide a crunchy accompaniment.

PER SERVING: 85 calories, 3 g fat

1 cucumber, topped, tailed and peeled
300 ml (½ pint) 'light' Greek-style natural yogurt
salt and freshly ground black pepper
freshly grated nutmeg
1 sachet powdered gelatine (see notes on gelatine page 72)
1 vegetable stock cube

TO SERVE:
1 bunch of watercress, stems trimmed
175 g (6 oz) prawns, defrosted naturally (if frozen) and well drained
1 lemon, cut into 6 wedges

1 Grate the cucumber, either in a food processor or by hand over a large bowl. Stir in the yogurt, salt, pepper and grated nutmeg.
2 Put 300 ml (½ pint) water, the gelatine and stock cube in a small saucepan. Warm over a very low heat, stirring until it is melted and clear. Leave to cool for 5 minutes.
3 Add the gelatine to the cucumber mixture, stirring and mixing well. Taste to check the seasoning, and pour into a soufflé dish or six ramekins.
4 Leave in the fridge to set for 2 hours. Remove from the fridge an hour before eating. Serve with the watercress, prawns and lemon wedges.

MAKES 4
PREPARATION & COOKING TIME:
10 minutes + about 40 minutes rising
+ 20 minutes cooking
FREEZING: recommended

PER SERVING: 494 calories, 9 g fat

These breads are **easy to make** and delicious to eat. Be sure to use easy bake yeast. Instead of making four large breads you can make 8 small ones or 2 rolls.

250 g (9 oz) strong white flour
250 g (9 oz) plain wholemeal flour
1 teaspoon fennel seeds
1 teaspoon salt
1 sachet (7 g) easy bake yeast
300 ml (11 fl oz) milk
1 teaspoon clear honey
1 tablespoon olive oil

1   Put the flours, fennel seeds, salt and yeast in a large bowl and mix together well. Whisk together the milk and honey, and add to the flour mixture.
2   Using one hand, mix the dough together. It should form into a ball, being neither too wet nor too crumbly and dry, and should leave the sides of the bowl completely clean. Add a little extra milk if necessary.
3   Knead for about 5 minutes until silky and smooth. Put in a clean bowl, pour over the oil, cover, and leave in a warm place until the dough has risen and doubled in size.
4   Preheat the oven to Gas Mark 7/electric oven 220°C/fan oven 200°C.
5   Divide the dough into 4 or 8 (or into small rolls), and knead each piece into a ball. With a rolling pin roll each ball into a circle approximately 17 cm (6½ inches).
6   Put on an oiled baking sheet and cook in the oven until well browned, about 15–20 minutes. Turn each bread over for the last 5 minutes. Tap the bottom of each bread to see if it is cooked through: it should sound hollow. Cool on a wire rack.
7   Serve the flatbreads as they are, with soup, or toasted and topped with olive oil.

FENNEL FLATBREAD

SERVES 4
PREPARATION TIME: 35 minutes
FREEZING: not recommended

A great snack or starter, which **can also be served as 'nibbles'** with drinks. Other vegetable suggestions for the crudités include: radishes, yellow/orange peppers, baby sweetcorn, courgettes, French beans, cherry tomatoes or fennel.

BUTTER BEAN DIP WITH CRUDITÉS

PER SERVING: 205 calories, 16 g fat

FOR THE DIP
200 g can of butter beans, rinsed and drained
1 or 2 garlic cloves, halved
4 tablespoons olive oil
juice of $1/2$ lemon
salt and freshly ground black pepper

FOR THE CRUDITÉS
2 carrots
3 celery sticks
1 green pepper, halved, de-seeded and
  white pith removed
1 red pepper, halved, de-seeded and
  white pith removed
3 spring onions, trimmed and halved
$1/2$ cucumber, quartered lengthways
  and seeds removed

1 Put all the dip ingredients in a food processor, and whizz until smooth. If too thick add a little water. Taste to check the seasoning, and spoon into a deep bowl.
2 To prepare the crudités, use a sharp knife to cut the vegetables into neat evenly sized sticks. Arrange around the bowl of dip.

SERVES 4
PREPARATION & COOKING TIME:
25 minutes
FREEZING: recommended

These pancakes are quite different. They use chick pea flour (found in the supermarket or specialist Indian shops), which gives a **really nutty authentic flavour**. Serve with the Coconut Vegetable Curry (page 52) or instead of tortillas (page 59). They are also very good on their own with plain yogurt and more fresh coriander.

CHICK PEA FLOUR PANCAKES

PER SERVING: 165 calories, 8 g fat

150 ml ($^1/_4$ pint) semi skimmed milk
125 g (4$^1/_2$ oz) chick pea (gram or besan) flour
salt and freshly ground black pepper
2 tablespoons chopped fresh coriander
1–2 tablespoons sunflower oil

1 Mix 150 ml ($^1/_4$ pint) water with the milk. Put the flour into a bowl and gradually add the liquid, beating well with a wooden spoon. The consistency of the batter needs to be like double cream. Season with salt and pepper and add the coriander.

2 Heat a couple of drops of oil in a small non-stick frying pan, pour in half a ladle of batter and quickly tilt the pan to spread the mixture.

3 Cook for about a minute on one side and either toss the pancake or flip it over with a palette knife and cook for another minute until golden on both sides. Use the remaining batter to make 7 more pancakes in the same way.

SERVES 4
PREPARATION TIME: 1 hour soaking + 15 minutes
FREEZING: not recommended

SERVES 4
PREPARATION & COOKING TIME:
10 minutes + 40 minutes cooking
FREEZING: not recommended

CHICORY & ORANGE SALAD

Chicory is sometimes bitter, but soaking it in cold water makes it less strong. This makes a very refreshing salad which is **particularly good with cold chicken**.

PER SERVING: 43 calories, 0 g fat

4 heads of chicory
2 oranges
salt and freshly ground black pepper

1   Trim the base of the chicory with a stainless steel knife, and cut into slices crossways. Put in a bowl, cover with cold water and leave to soak for at least an hour.
2   With a sharp knife (a serrated one is best) peel the oranges over a serving bowl to reserve the juice, removing all the white pith with the peel.
3   Cut the oranges into slices or segments, removing any pips, and place in the bowl with the juice. Drain the chicory well and add to the oranges with a little salt and lots of black pepper.

SWEET POTATO CHIPS

If you have not tried sweet potatoes before, these 'chips' are a good way to start. They make a great **late night snack**.

PER SERVING: 169 calories, 8 g fat

450 g (1 lb) sweet potatoes, thinly peeled
2 tablespoons olive oil
2 teaspoons fennel seeds
1 teaspoon chilli powder or garam massala
salt

1   Preheat the oven to Gas Mark 6/electric oven 200°C/fan oven 180°C.
2   Cut the potatoes into chunky chips and put in a large bowl. Add the oil and mix well so that all the chips are well coated.
3   Spread on a baking sheet (not a deep tray) and sprinkle over the fennel seeds and chilli powder or garam massala.
4   Cook in the oven for 30–35 minutes until the chips are golden and crispy.
5   Serve immediately with a little salt sprinkled over.

SERVES 4
PREPARATION TIME: 10 minutes
FREEZING: not suitable

LETTUCE & CELERY WITH A CREAMY DRESSING

This creamy dressing is a simple variation on 'regular' salad dressing, but is quite **different and delicious!**

PER SERVING: 119 calories, 11 g fat

2 Little Gem lettuces or 1 Cos lettuce
4 leafy celery sticks, chopped into chunks
2 tablespoons low fat crème fraîche
1 teaspoon Dijon mustard
1 teaspoon caster sugar
salt and freshly ground black pepper
2 tablespoons good quality olive oil
2 tablespoons tarragon vinegar

1   Cut the lettuce into thick slices, and put with the celery in a deep salad bowl.
2   In a small bowl, blend together the crème fraîche, mustard, sugar, salt and pepper. Using a small whisk, beat in the olive oil, drop by drop.
3   When all the oil has been absorbed, stir in the vinegar until the dressing has the consistency of thick cream.
4   Pour over the lettuce and celery, toss well to mix, and serve immediately.

SERVES 4
PREPARATION & COOKING TIME: 30 minutes
FREEZING: not recommended

WARM POTATO SALAD WITH CAPERS

This potato salad is a little different and **very easy to make**. It can also be served cold.

PER SERVING: 164 calories, 8 g fat

450g (1lb) small waxy new potatoes, unpeeled
1/4 red onion, chopped finely
1 tablespoon capers, drained and chopped
2 tablespoons olive oil
2 teaspoons dried dill
salt and freshly ground black pepper

1   Cut the potatoes into bite size pieces, cover with salted water and simmer for about 10 minutes until just soft.
2   Meanwhile, put the onion, capers, oil, dill, salt and pepper in a salad bowl.
3   Drain the potatoes well and put hot into the salad bowl with the other ingredients. Stir to mix, cover and leave until just warm.

You may use any type of pasta for the recipes given here. I prefer to use dried pasta, as I find that fresh pasta can be a little 'damp' and is also easy to overcook. Dried pasta will keep in the store cupboard for ages, and will always be there to rustle up a quick and healthy meal, rather than resorting to a calorie-rich take away. The pasta sauces are all easy to make, and are so much better than any from the inevitable tin or packet, particularly the Tomato and Basil – try it and compare.

PASTA & FISH

When you can get good fresh fish (do patronise your fishmonger, if you have one), it is best eaten straight away. Fish can be frozen, but not for much longer than 4 weeks as it suffers from 'freezer burn'. Dealing with the skin and bones is something that puts a lot of people off eating fish, but the fishmonger will always remove these for you. Cooking fish 'en papillote' (in a foil parcel) is a quick and easy method. You can then add any of your favourite flavours.

SERVES 4
PREPARATION & COOKING TIME:
10 minutes + 20 minutes cooking
FREEZING: not recommended

PER SERVING: 405 calories, 9 g fat

This pasta dish is simple, and has a very **light and fresh taste**. Do not boil the tomato sauce – this will keep the basil as green and as flavourful as possible.

4 fresh plum tomatoes
350 g (12 oz) fettuccine
25 g (1 oz) fresh basil,
leaves removed from the stalks
2 tablespoons good olive oil
salt and freshly ground black pepper
freshly shaved half fat Parmesan cheese,
to serve

1 Skin the tomatoes: put them in a bowl, pour over boiling water, leave for 1 minute, then drain off the water. You will now be able to remove the skins easily. Use a sharp pointed knife to remove the core where the stalk was attached.
2 Bring a large pan of salted water to the boil and cook the pasta until just soft (al dente).
3 Meanwhile, chop the tomatoes roughly, saving all the juices, and put in a bowl. Lightly shred the basil leaves and add with the oil to the tomatoes. Season with salt and pepper.
4 When the pasta is cooked, drain well, reserving 150 ml (¼ pint) of the cooking liquid. Return the liquid to the saucepan, add the tomato mixture, and reheat without boiling.
5 Add the drained pasta, check the seasoning, and quickly stir to mix. Divide between four pasta dishes and serve with freshly shaved Parmesan to sprinkle over.

FETTUCCINE WITH TOMATO & BASIL

SERVES 4
PREPARATION & COOKING TIME:
10 minutes + 25 minutes cooking
FREEZING: not recommended

SERVES 4
PREPARATION & COOKING TIME:
10 minutes + 15 minutes cooking
FREEZING: not recommended

PENNE WITH RED PEPPERS & BROCCOLI

TAGLIATELLE WITH WILD MUSHROOMS

The red peppers and broccoli make a **really good combination** with the pasta. Do make sure to cook the peppers very slowly, and in a heavy based saucepan.

PER SERVING: 450 calories, 13 g fat

2 large red peppers, halved and de-seeded
3 tablespoons olive oil
1 garlic clove, crushed
salt and freshly ground black pepper
125 g (4¹/₂ oz) broccoli florets, trimmed
350 g (12 oz) penne
freshly grated half fat Parmesan cheese, to serve

1   Cut each of the pepper halves into two, remove the white pith, and cut into slices. Heat the oil in a heavy based saucepan, add the garlic, peppers, salt and pepper, and stir to mix well.
2   Turn the heat to its lowest and put on the saucepan lid. Cook for about 20 minutes until the peppers are really soft and have almost made a sauce.
3   Meanwhile, bring a large saucepan of salted water to the boil and cook the broccoli for 5 minutes until just tender. Remove with a slotted spoon and add to the peppers.
4   Cook the pasta in the broccoli water until just soft (al dente). Drain well and return to the large saucepan. Add the pepper mixture, stir to mix well, and serve immediately with freshly grated Parmesan.

You often see 'exotic' or 'wild' mushrooms in the supermarket, this is a good opportunity to try them. They have **a lot more flavour** than regular mushrooms, but if you can't find them, any other mushrooms will do.

PER SERVING: 381 calories, 18 g fat

350 g (12 oz) tagliatelle
4 tablespoons olive oil
2 fat garlic cloves, sliced thinly
175 g (6 oz) wild mushrooms, chopped roughly
salt and freshly ground black pepper
2 tablespoons chopped fresh parsley

1   Cook the pasta in a large saucepan of boiling salted water until just soft (al dente).
2   Meanwhile, heat the oil in a small saucepan and fry the garlic slices until just beginning to brown.
3   Add the mushrooms to the garlic and cook for 4–5minutes until the mushrooms soften and release their juices. Season with salt and pepper.
4   Drain the pasta, return to the saucepan and pour over the mushroom mixture. Stir to mix and sprinkle in the parsley. Serve immediately.

SERVES 4
PREPARATION & COOKING TIME:
5 minutes + 15 minutes cooking
FREEZING: not recommended

SPAGHETTI WITH OLIVE OIL, GARLIC & CHILLI

This is a very **simple and classic** recipe for pasta, which can be 'rustled up' quickly with store cupboard ingredients.

PER SERVING: 440 calories, 15 g fat

350 g (12 oz) spaghetti
4 tablespoons olive oil
2 garlic cloves, crushed
1 teaspoon chilli flakes
salt
freshly grated half fat Parmesan cheese, to serve

1 Cook the spaghetti in a large saucepan of boiling salted water until just soft (al dente).
2 Meanwhile, put the oil, garlic and chilli flakes in a small saucepan and warm over a low heat to release the flavours into the oil. Season with salt.
3 Drain the pasta, and return to the saucepan. Pour over the oil and chilli mixture, and stir together to mix. Serve immediately with freshly grated Parmesan.

SERVES 4
PREPARATION & COOKING TIME: 15 minutes
FREEZING: not recommended

OAT CRUSTED SALMON

Using low fat cooking spray oil (available in the supermarket) and a non-stick pan makes this fish lovely and **crusty on the outside** while only using very little oil. The lemon juice makes a perfect accompaniment, and new potatoes and a green vegetable would complete the dish.

PER SERVING: 317 calories, 19 g fat

600 g (1 lb 5oz) salmon fillet, skinned
    (ask the fishmonger to do this for you)
2 tablespoons porridge oats
2 teaspoons sesame seeds
salt and freshly ground black pepper
cooking spray sunflower oil
1 large lemon, cut into 4, to serve

1 Cut the salmon into four evenly sized pieces. On a plate mix together the oats, sesame seeds, salt and pepper.
2 Dip each salmon portion into the oat mixture, and press in to coat all over. The dampness of the fish will make the mixture stick.
3 Heat a non-stick frying pan, spray in the oil and put in the salmon. Cook over a medium heat for about 3 minutes on each side, covering with a lid. The fish will be brown and crispy on the outside, and the lid will provide steam to help it cook through.
4 Serve with the lemon wedges.

SERVES 4
PREPARATION & COOKING TIME:
15 minutes + 25 minutes cooking
FREEZING: not recommended

PER SERVING: 163 calories, 6 g fat

This is a lovely recipe, half way between a stew and a soup. It's **very nourishing** and filling.

SMOKED HADDOCK STEW

300 ml (^{1}/$_2$ pint) boiling water
225 g (8 oz) smoked haddock fillet
1 tablespoon sunflower oil
1 onion, sliced finely
2 celery sticks, chopped finely
1 carrot, sliced finely
1 potato, peeled and diced finely
^{1}/$_2$ teaspoon turmeric powder
1 sprig fresh thyme
2 fresh bay leaves
salt and freshly ground black pepper
300 ml (^{1}/$_2$ pint) semi skimmed milk
75 g (2^3/$_4$ oz) frozen peas
freshly ground nutmeg

1 Pour the boiling water over the haddock. Leave for 5 minutes, drain and reserve the liquid.

2 Heat the oil in a saucepan and gently fry the onion for 2 minutes. Add the celery, carrot and potato and continue to fry for 2 more minutes. Add half the reserved fish stock, the turmeric, thyme, bay leaves and salt and pepper.

3 Bring to the boil and simmer very gently with the lid on, until the vegetables are soft, about 15 minutes. Add the rest of the stock, the milk and peas.

4 Cook for a further 3 minutes. Gently flake in the fish, remove the bay leaves and thyme, and grate in a little nutmeg. Taste to check the seasoning before serving.

SERVES 4
PREPARATION & COOKING TIME: 25 minutes
FREEZING: not recommended

POACHED WHITE FISH WITH GREEN SALSA

This is a very simple and delicious recipe which could be used for **any white fish**. The green chilli adds only a little heat, but you can use half a chilli or leave it out completely if preferred. Serve the fish with new potatoes and a green vegetable.

PER SERVING: 287 calories, 15 g fat

FOR THE FISH
4 x 175 g (6 oz) portions of white fish (turbot, brill, halibut, skate wing), skinned
1/2 small onion, sliced
2 tablespoons white wine vinegar
salt and freshly ground black pepper

FOR THE SALSA
3 tablespoons olive oil
grated zest and juice of 1 lime
1 fresh green chilli, de-seeded and finely chopped
2 tablespoons chopped fresh coriander

1 Put the fish into a shallow pan, just cover with water and add the onion, vinegar, salt and pepper. Bring to the boil and simmer for 3 minutes.
2 Turn off the heat, and leave to stand for 10 minutes. Remove the fish with a fish slice and drain on kitchen towel. Put on a plate and keep warm.
3 For the salsa, heat the oil gently in a small saucepan. Add the lime zest and juice, the chilli and coriander. Allow to bubble up, then pour over the fish.
4 Serve immediately.

SERVES 4
PREPARATION & COOKING TIME: 45 minutes
FREEZING: not recommended

PRAWNS WITH TOMATO & CARAWAY

This may seem to be a very **unusual combination of flavours**, but it really works and tastes wonderful. Serve with a green salad and some crusty bread to mop up the juices.

PER SERVING: 153 calories, 8 g fat

2 tablespoons olive oil
2 garlic cloves, sliced finely
1 teaspoon caraway seeds
1 or 2 dried red chillies, crumbled
1 green pepper, de-seeded and chopped finely
400 g can of chopped tomatoes
salt and freshly ground black pepper
a pinch of sugar
350 g (12 oz) prawns, defrosted naturally (if frozen) and well drained
1 tablespoon chopped fresh coriander

1   Heat the oil in a medium saucepan and fry the sliced garlic until just golden. Add the caraway seeds, chillies and green pepper, and stir well.
2   Add the tomatoes, salt and pepper and sugar. Simmer for 20 minutes until the pepper is soft and the sauce thickened.
3   Add the prawns and reheat for 3 minutes. Serve immediately, sprinkled with chopped coriander.

SERVES 4
PREPARATION & COOKING TIME: 20 minutes
FREEZING: not recommended

HAKE BAKED EN PAPILLOTE

This is a really good way of cooking fish: the sealed foil 'packets' **keep in the flavours**, and save on the washing up. You can substitute sliced tomatoes, chopped coriander or a little garlic for the olives – experiment as much as you want.

PER SERVING: 184 calories, 6 g fat

4 x 175 g (6 oz) portions of hake or haddock, skinned
12 black olives, stoned and chopped roughly
finely grated zest of 1 lemon
freshly ground black pepper
a little olive oil
4 fresh bay leaves (optional)

1   Preheat the oven to Gas Mark 5/electric oven 190°C/fan oven 170°C.
2   Lay each portion of fish on a large square of aluminium foil, sprinkle on the chopped olives and lemon zest and season with pepper.
3   Put on a flat baking sheet, sprinkle a little olive oil over each one and top with a bay leaf, if used. Scrunch up each foil parcel tightly.
4   Bake in the preheated oven for 15 minutes.
5   Serve the wrapped parcels as they are – open them up on your plate and let the juices run out.

All of these vegetarian recipes are suitable as main courses. They are delicious and wholesome and are suitable for the bored meat-eater as well as true vegetarians. Why not try having a meat-free meal at least once a week? These

VEGETARIAN

recipes might help to convert you and your family. On the other hand, the Coconut Curry works just as well using skinless, diced chicken breasts instead of the vegetables – the choice is yours.

SERVES 4
PREPARATION & COOKING TIME:
15 minutes + 40 minutes cooking
FREEZING: not recommended

PER SERVING: 242 calories, 16 g fat

This is really good. It can be eaten warm with lots of crusty bread to mop up the juices, or as a vegetable to accompany a main course. If you like lots of **chilli heat**, leave in the chilli seeds. You can also serve the squash cold, but I think warm is better. Other types of squash or pumpkin can be prepared in the same way.

**2 butternut squash,
about 1 kg (2 lb 4 oz), peeled
3 tablespoons olive oil
salt
2 tablespoons sesame seeds
4 spring onions, chopped finely
2 tablespoons chopped fresh coriander
1 medium hot fresh red chilli,
de-seeded and chopped finely
juice of ½ lemon**

1 Preheat the oven to Gas Mark 6/electric oven 200°C/fan oven 180°C.
2 Cut the squash into quarters and remove the seeds. Chop into bite size chunks and put into a roasting tin with the oil and some salt. Mix well so that all the pieces are coated in oil.
3 Roast in the oven for about 30–40 minutes until just tender, but still firm and not mushy.
4 Meanwhile toast/dry fry the sesame seeds in a small frying pan. Keep shaking the pan, taking care not to burn them. They will begin to smell nutty and become golden in colour.
5 Cool the squash and all the cooking juices in a large bowl for 10 minutes. Add all the other ingredients, mix well and add more salt to taste, if necessary.

ROASTED BUTTERNUT SQUASH

SERVES 6
PREPARATION & COOKING TIME:
1¹/₂ hours
FREEZING: not recommended

PER SERVING: 235 calories, 2 g fat

400 g can of chopped tomatoes
1 vegetable stock cube
1 garlic clove, crushed
1–2 dried red chillies,
more if you like it really hot
salt and freshly ground black pepper

175 g (6 oz) couscous (page 62),
(omit cumin if preferred)
2 tablespoons chopped fresh parsley

FOR THE VEGETABLES:
225 g (8 oz) small new potatoes,
scrubbed and halved lengthways
2 carrots, cut into large sticks
1 small white cabbage,
cut into 8 and the core removed
1 onion, cut into chunks
1 turnip, cut into chunks
1 parsnip, cut into chunks
175 g (6 oz) shelled fresh broad beans
4 celery sticks, scrubbed and cut into chunks
1 small aubergine, cut into chunks
1 small sweet potato, peeled
and cut into chunks
¹/₂ butternut squash, peeled, seeds removed
and cut into chunks

Traditionally in Morocco a **selection of seven vegetables** is used in this dish – seven is considered to be a lucky number. Choose any seven from those listed below, the choice is yours. The secret is to cook whichever vegetables you select in the right order, so follow the sequence of cooking given here.

1   Put the tomatoes, 300 ml (¹/₂ pint) water, the stock cube, garlic, chillies, salt and pepper In a large saucepan and bring to the boil.
2   Add the vegetables in rotation, starting with the new potatoes, carrots, cabbage and onion. Cover and simmer for 10 minutes.
3   Next add the turnip, parsnip, broad beans and celery, and cook for a further 10 minutes.
4   Lastly add the aubergine, sweet potato and squash and cook for another 10 minutes.
5   Meanwhile, make up the couscous and turn on to a large serving plate. Using a slotted spoon, pile the vegetables into the centre of the dish.
6   Ladle over a little of the spicy stock and sprinkle with the chopped parsley. Serve the rest of the stock separately in a sauce boat.

VEGETABLE COUSCOUS

SERVES 4
PREPARATION & COOKING TIME:
40 minutes + 1 hour cooling
FREEZING: recommended

PER BURGER: 230 calories, 12 g fat

These spicy burgers make a great **healthy alternative to meat burgers**, and can be served in a wholemeal bun with red onion slices and salad if you prefer.

2 x 400 g cans of chick peas, rinsed and drained
2 tablespoons olive oil
1 small onion, chopped finely
1 garlic clove, crushed
1 red pepper, de-seeded and finely chopped
2 tablespoons chopped fresh coriander
1 fresh red chilli, de-seeded and finely chopped
salt and freshly ground black pepper
a little sunflower oil or cooking spray to fry the burgers
tomato salsa (page 59), to serve

1 Put the chick peas into a food processor, and pulse two or three times to lightly mix – you do not want them to be mushy but to retain some texture. Turn into a large bowl.
2 Heat the olive oil and gently fry the onion, garlic and pepper for 5 minutes to soften. Add to the chick peas, with the coriander, chilli, salt and pepper.
3 Stir to mix well and cool in the fridge for at least 1 hour, or overnight. Divide the mixture into 8 and shape into burgers (you may need a little flour to do this).
4 Heat the sunflower oil or cooking spray in a non-stick frying pan and fry the burgers for 3 minutes on each side until they are golden and crispy.
5 Drain on kitchen towel. Serve warm with the tomato salsa.

CHICK PEA BURGERS WITH TOMATO SALSA

COCONUT VEGETABLE CURRY

This is a straightforward and **simple vegetable curry**. If you prefer, you can make it hotter by adding an extra chilli or more curry paste. Serve with rice or Chick Pea Flour Pancakes (page 33).

PER SERVING: 219 calories, 16 g fat

1 onion, chopped
1 potato, peeled and cut into chunks
1 small aubergine, cut into chunks
1 carrot, cut into chunks
1 small red pepper, de-seeded and chopped
1 small green pepper, de-seeded and chopped
2 garlic cloves, crushed
1 fresh green or red chilli, de-seeded and chopped finely
a walnut-sized piece of fresh ginger, peeled and chopped finely
2 tablespoons good quality curry paste (medium or hot)
75 g (2¾ oz) creamed coconut, chopped
juice of ½ lemon
2 tablespoons chopped fresh coriander
salt

1 Put all the vegetables with the garlic, chilli and ginger in a large saucepan, and cover with water (about 300–350 ml/10–12 fl oz). Bring to the boil and stir in the curry paste.
2 Simmer gently until the vegetables are tender, about 20 minutes, adding a little more water if needed.
3 Add the creamed coconut, stirring gently to mix, then add the lemon juice, coriander and salt. Taste to check the seasoning and serve.

SERVES 4 as a vegetable, 2 as a main course
PREPARATION & COOKING TIME: 30 minutes
FREEZING: not recommended

SERVES 3
PREPARATION & COOKING TIME: 20 minutes
FREEZING: not recommended

MEGADARRA

BUTTER BEANS ON TOAST

This recipe is based on a medieval dish from the Middle East and is sometimes known as 'Esau's favourite'. Though simple to make, the **mixture of rice and lentils** really works, and the caramelised onions add a wonderful flavour. Plain yogurt makes a good accompaniment.

PER (MAIN) SERVING: 607 calories, 31 g fat

125 g (4¹/₂ oz) long grain rice
400 g can of brown lentils, rinsed and drained
3 onions, halved and sliced finely
4 tablespoons olive oil
salt and freshly ground black pepper

1 Cook the rice in boiling salted water for 12–15 minutes until just soft. Drain well and mix together with the lentils in a serving dish.
2 Meanwhile, fry the onions in the oil until they are dark brown and beginning to caramelise. Add to the rice and lentils.
3 Rinse out the hot frying pan with 2 tablespoons of water, swill it around to loosen all the last bits of browned onion and add to the rice mixture.
4 Season and stir well with a fork to mix. Serve warm.

A really **interesting take on baked beans on toast**, especially with the watercress adding extra vitamins.

PER SERVING: 279 calories, 16 g fat

400 g can of butter beans, rinsed and drained
2 spring onions, trimmed and chopped finely
2 teaspoons coarse-grain French mustard
¹/₂ bunch of watercress, trimmed and chopped roughly
a few drops of Tabasco sauce
3 tablespoons olive oil
salt and freshly ground black pepper
3 slices of bread (wholemeal, granary or other interesting type)

1 Put the butter beans in a bowl and mash lightly to break up some of the beans. Add the spring onions, mustard, watercress, Tabasco and 2 tablespoons of olive oil. Season with salt and pepper.
2 Using the grill, lightly toast the bread on both sides. Spread the bean mixture evenly over the toast making sure you cover the edges to prevent burning.
3 Put the toast back under a medium grill and cook for 6–7 minutes until the topping is just golden. Serve immediately with the remaining olive oil sprinkled over the top.

SERVES 6
PREPARATION & COOKING TIME:
20 minutes + 30 minutes cooking
FREEZING: recommended

PER SERVING: 265 calories, 13 g fat

This is a savoury tart tatin – really an **upside down tomato pie**. With good-flavoured tomatoes, it makes an unusual supper or light lunch dish.

TOMATO TART TATIN

225 g (8 oz) plain flour
1 heaped teaspoon baking powder
salt and freshly ground black pepper
50 g (1³/₄ oz) butter
150 ml (¹/₄ pint) semi skimmed milk
450 g (1 lb) plum tomatoes,
or other good-flavoured vine tomatoes
2 tablespoons olive oil
1 teaspoon dried basil
8 fresh basil leaves, to garnish

1 Sieve the flour and baking powder into a large bowl. Season with salt and pepper. Rub in the fat using just your fingertips. Add the milk to make a soft dough, and set aside.
2 Meanwhile, skin the tomatoes (page 38) and cut each one into three thick slices.
3 Preheat the oven to Gas Mark 7/electric oven 220°C/fan oven 200°C.
4 Put the oil into a shallow, round ovenproof dish about 24 cm (9¹/₂ inches) in diameter. Lay the tomatoes on the bottom of the dish, sprinkle over the dried basil, salt and pepper.
5 Roll the dough out to fit over the tomatoes, put on top and tuck the edges inside the dish to seal. Cook in the oven for about 30 minutes until the crust is well risen and golden.
6 Remove from the oven, and release the edges with a knife. Leave to cool for 4 minutes, then turn upside down on to a serving dish. Scatter over the fresh torn basil, and serve warm.

You will see that most of the meat recipes use chicken or beef. This is because pork and lamb are usually very fatty, and not suitable for a low calorie diet. Most of the fat in a chicken is in the skin, and it is important to remove as much of the skin as you can before you start cooking. This is

CHICKEN & MEAT

where all the flavourings mentioned in the Introduction come into play. Use as much or as little as you wish. You will find when using chillies that the more you eat, the higher your heat tolerance becomes.

SERVES 4
PREPARATION & COOKING TIME:
10 minutes + 2 hours marinating + 40 minutes cooking
FREEZING: not recommended

GRILLED CHICKEN THIGHS WITH LEMON, MUSTARD & THYME

Served with a green salad, this makes **a great supper or lunch**. The chicken is also good served cold. The pieces of lemon can be eaten as well, the juices will 'leak' into the potatoes — it's delicious.

PER SERVING: 435 calories, 19 g fat

8 chicken thighs, all skin and fat removed
2 tablespoons olive oil
1 tablespoon Dijon mustard
1 lemon, cut into 4
a large sprig of thyme, broken into 4
2 garlic cloves, crushed
salt and freshly ground black pepper700 g (1 lb 9 oz) new potatoes, unpeeled

1. Put the chicken and all the other ingredients except the potatoes, into a large bowl. Mix well so that all the chicken thighs are coated. Cover and leave to marinate in the fridge for at least 2 hours or overnight.
2. Preheat the grill and the oven to Gas Mark 6/electric oven 200°C/fan oven 180°C.
3. Put the chicken and all the marinade ingredients into a shallow dish or tray. Grill for 10 minutes on each side until golden and crispy.
4. Put into the oven for 20 minutes to finish cooking all the way through. Meanwhile, cook the potatoes in boiling water, drain well and crush lightly.
5. Put the potatoes on a serving dish, pile the chicken and the marinade on top and serve.

SERVES 4
PREPARATION & COOKING TIME: 55 minutes
FREEZING: not recommended

SPICY CHICKEN TORTILLA WRAPS

Tortilla wraps are great fun **for all the family**. Serve all the 'makings' in separate bowls and then the 'wrapping' can be done at the table, and everyone can choose their own fillings.

PER SERVING: 488 calories, 14 g fat

FOR THE TOMATO SALSA:
2 tomatoes, skins removed and chopped finely
1 fresh green chilli, de-seeded and chopped finely
$\frac{1}{2}$ small onion, chopped finely
1 tablespoon chopped fresh coriander
1 tablespoon olive oil
salt

1 teaspoon ground cumin
a good pinch of chilli powder
1 dessertspoon sunflower oil
4 skinless chicken breasts, cut into strips
juice of 1 lime
salt

TO SERVE:
8 tortillas
200 g pot of low fat plain yogurt

1 Mix all the salsa ingredients together, cover and leave to stand for at least 20 minutes.
2 Mix together the cumin and chilli powder and sprinkle over the chicken. Heat the oil in a non-stick frying pan, add the spiced chicken and stir fry on a high heat for 10 minutes.
3 Add the lime juice and salt to taste and keep warm.
4 Meanwhile, wrap the tortillas in a tea towel and heat in the microwave for 2 minutes on High.
5 Place everything in separate dishes and let everyone make their own wraps with the tortillas, chicken, salsa and yogurt.

SERVES 4
PREPARATION & COOKING TIME:
15 minutes + 15 minutes cooking
FREEZING: not recommended

PER SERVING: 237 calories, 10 g fat

This recipe is inspired by classic **Thai green curries**, but they contain lots more coconut – and lots more calories. You can buy Thai spice packs from the supermarket, which saves buying all the ingredients separately. Lemon grass gives an authentic flavour; to prepare it for this recipe, top and tail and remove the outer woody layers. If you like your curry mild use one chilli, for a hotter taste use two. Serve with basmati rice.

2 garlic cloves, halved
1 lemon grass stalk, trimmed and cut into 3
1 or 2 fresh green chillies,
halved and de-seeded
5 cm (2 inches) fresh ginger, peeled
and chopped roughly
25 g (1 oz) fresh coriander,
tough stalks removed
1 tablespoon sunflower oil
1 small onion, halved and sliced finely
4 skinless chicken breasts,
cut into bite size pieces
salt
1 chicken stock cube
50 g (1³/₄ oz) creamed coconut

1 Put the garlic, lemon grass, chilli, ginger, coriander and 300 ml (½ pint) cold water Into the food processor. Process for 2–3 minutes until well mixed.
2 Heat the oil in a non-stick frying pan and add the onion. Fry for 2 minutes then add the chicken. Stir fry for 3–4 minutes, add the coriander mixture, salt and crumbled stock cube.
3 Bring up to the boil stirring well, turn down the heat, cover, and cook for 10 minutes.
4 Add the coconut, and stir until melted and well mixed. Taste to check the seasoning.

GREEN CHICKEN CURRY